A Pilgrim's Guide to

IONA ABBEY

First published 2006 by
Wild Goose Publications,
4th Floor, Savoy House, 140 Sauchiehall St, Glasgow G2 3DH, UK.
Wild Goose Publications is the publishing division of the Iona Community.
Scottish Charity No. SC003794. Limited Company Reg. No. SC096243.
www.ionabooks.com

ISBN 1-905010-12-5
13-digit ISBN: 978-1-905010-12-7

A catalogue record for this book is available from the British Library.

Overseas distribution:
Australia: Willow Connection Pty Ltd, Unit 4A, 3-9 Kenneth Road, Manly Vale, NSW 2093
New Zealand: Pleroma, Higginson Street, Otane 4170, Central Hawkes Bay
Canada: Novalis/Bayard Publishing & Distribution, 10 Lower Spadina Ave., Suite 400, Toronto, Ontario M5V 2Z2

Printed by Bell & Bain, Thornliebank, Glasgow

A Pilgrim's Guide to

IONA ABBEY

WILD GOOSE PUBLICATIONS

'Iona is a thin place – only a tissue paper separates the spiritual from the material.'

Revd. George MacLeod
Founder of the Iona Community

INTRODUCTION

Welcome to Iona. You may have come across the sound from the Ross of Mull just for the day, or you may be staying here for a week in one of the Christian centres on the island: at Bishop's House; the House of Prayer, Cnoc a' Chalmain; Duncraig; or in the Abbey or the MacLeod Centre. Maybe you have come to enjoy an island holiday. Whatever has brought you, you are one of thousands of folk who come to Iona every year; one of millions who have been here over the centuries.

The fabric of the church and other parts of the site are looked after by Historic Scotland. So the best way to get a sense of the Abbey's history and architecture is to take one of the Historic Scotland guided tours around the buildings. Times of these tours are available at the entrance kiosk.

Iona is also a place where people come looking for answers – to get in touch with their spiritual needs and find a new vision of themselves and their lives, and of our lives together. So perhaps this journey to Iona is a pilgrimage for you – or perhaps you would like to become a pilgrim now. Once you have got your bearings in the Abbey, we hope you'll be able to spend a little longer here and connect with the meanings and purpose of this place. At 2 pm (in the summertime) the Iona Community holds a short service of prayers for justice and peace, which you are very welcome to join.

This pilgrim's guide has been prepared by members of the Iona Community. It gives you an opportunity to walk around the Abbey church and cloisters with suggestions for reflection and prayer. There are also some stories from Iona Community members. At each point you will find:

- some background information
- something to think about
- a simple prayer

We hope that when you get home again, the sights and sounds of Iona, rain or shine, will stay with you, and that this little book will help you to use your memories as the starting point for prayer.

As new guests and visitors arrive each week, the Iona Community holds a service of welcome in the Abbey church. At the service this Celtic rune of hospitality is often said:

We saw a stranger yesterday,
We put food in the eating place,
Drink in the drinking place,
Music in the listening place
And, with the sacred name of the Triune God,
He blessed us and our house,
Our cattle and our dear ones.

As the lark says in her song:
Often, often, often goes Christ in the stranger's guise.

From *Iona Abbey Worship Book*

ST MARTIN'S CROSS

Begin your pilgrim walk outside the Abbey church at St Martin's Cross – the high stone cross in front of the main Abbey entrance.

Large Celtic crosses like this one were raised to proclaim the importance of a holy place. St Martin's Cross was raised outside the original, sixth-century Celtic church, and has stood on this spot for over twelve hundred years. It has stood the test of time because it is made from local epidiorite rock, which is very hard. A 'preaching cross', it has Bible stories carved on its west face, including Mary with the infant Jesus in the centre circle and, underneath this, Daniel in the lions' den and Abraham stopped from sacrificing Isaac. St Martin established the first monastery in Western Europe and his community became the model for religious communities in Ireland, Scotland and Wales. On this spot our Christian forebears gathered. Take a moment to think of them along with all the modern visitors who have come here, and all those who stand with you today.

At this starting place of your pilgrimage, recall a gospel story that has special meaning for you.

PRAYER

Holy Spirit,
awaken my heart
to the Good News you have for me today.
May the stones of this holy place shout aloud for you,
the Living God. Amen

A STORY

I remember being struck forcibly by a comment made by one Celtic scholar who said that the Celtic Church showed remarkable courage in being prepared to set not Christ alone at the centre of this cross but Jesus in the arms of Mary; I gather that this was very unusual. Mary had a very significant place in the devotion of the Celtic Church. Standing by her son at the foot of the cross, Mary suffered with him the most appalling anguish, and her part in God's scheme of salvation deserves to be recognised by the Church.

Graeme Brown, a member of the Iona Community

THE STREET OF THE DEAD

Near St Martin's Cross, you will see a cobbled road.

This medieval road ran from the harbour (Martyrs' Bay) to the Reilig Odhráin chapel, and on to the bakehouse. The bakehouse was sited on what is now the Peace Garden, and offered a practical welcome to travellers and pilgrims. Along the Street of the Dead were carried the coffins of kings and chieftains brought to the sacred isle of Iona for burial.

Stand on the Street of the Dead, and think of the things you would like to leave buried here; and of the food you need to keep you going.

Prayer

Eternal God,
You bring life out of death.
Take and hold
all I need to put behind me.
In my pilgrimage here
may I know Your sustaining love.
Amen

Look north for a rocky, grass-covered mound.

TÒRR AN ABA

This is believed to be the site of St Columba's wattled cell. There are clues in the *Life of St Columba*, written one hundred years after his death, which identify this place. Columba came to Iona from Ireland, possibly exiled after secretly copying a book of psalms (very rare and valuable then) and refusing to return the copy to the owner of the original book after the legal judgement went against him. A war between clans began. Many died; and Columba was exiled and told to win as many souls for Christ as had been lost in battle. It is just as possible that he came to Iona as a 'green martyr': someone who, for Christ's sake, leaves behind comforts and all they love most. Columba launched a great Christian mission, and many came to Iona for his counsel and wisdom. Many still come for inspiration.

Climb Tòrr an Aba, or stand beside it, and look out at the sea, land and sky that Columba would have seen every day; then look closely at the rock of Tòrr an Aba. Creation: God's 'big book'.

Prayer

May God's goodness be yours,
and well, and seven times well, may you spend your lives:
may you be an isle in the sea, may you be a hill on the shore,
may you be a star in the darkness, may you be a staff to the weak;
may the love Christ Jesus gave fill every heart for you;
may the love Christ Jesus gave fill you for every one.

Traditional Celtic prayer, from *Iona Abbey Worship Book*

Face the Abbey and look to your left; you'll see another high stone cross near the west door.

ST JOHN'S CROSS

St John's Cross stands outside St Columba's Shrine and proclaims the sacred place where St Columba was once buried. (Because of Viking raids, St Columba's bones were disinterred a century after burial.) St John was revered by the Celtic monks for his emphasis on mystical contemplation.

Sit or kneel in St Columba's Shrine, or stand beside St John's Cross, and, for a moment, find a quiet place within yourself.

Prayer

May the desire of my heart
be centred with God this day.

A STORY

One day in the 1960s, the morning post brought a chunky parcel for George MacLeod. We were all there, in the refectory, when he opened it. Inside was a brass candlestick, in three pieces, which could be screwed together – with a note saying it was a gift to the community, and that it was one of a pair from, I think, the travelling mass set of a Russian Orthodox bishop of a few centuries ago. George was delighted – because there already was another one, very similar, in St Columba's Shrine, and George was of course a great admirer of the Russian Orthodox Church. I was a volunteer then, and I happened to be standing near George when he opened the parcel. Turning to me, simply because I was nearest, he said, 'Come with me,' and led me downstairs and into the shrine. He assembled the candlestick, placed it on the communion table beside its twin, and then invited me to kneel with him in prayer. Very simply, he dedicated the candlestick, and both of us, there and then in that ancient shrine. It was an insight into the man that I had never had before; up till then, I had been rather in awe of him as a great public figure. I guess I remained somewhat in awe of him for the rest of his life – but I never forgot that simple prayer, in the shrine, with a young, green, and probably pretty confused volunteer!

John Harvey, a member of the Iona Community

Enter the Abbey church through the west door. Just inside the door, look left and up the narrow stairway.

THE WATCHING PLACE

In the thirteenth century, the Benedictines came to Iona and built the Abbey church on the site of the original Celtic church. In the watching place, one of the monks would be stationed both to guard the Abbey and to welcome approaching pilgrims. Hospitality was central to the ministry of the Benedictines and the Columban monks. It is central to the ministry of the Iona Community today.

You are welcome here.

Prayer

When we are happy,
when we are full of fun and laughter
God welcomes us.
When we are angry,
when people let us down and make us sad
God welcomes us.
When we are tired,
when we need to stop and
curl up and rest
God welcomes us.

A STORY

Of all the folk who turned up unannounced when we were here in the 1970s, the one I always remember was an octogenarian aristocratic Scotswoman who had been a Russian Orthodox nun in France for almost all her adult life. She'd gone there after the First World War, the daughter of a British admiral and the sister of a British general, to help look after Russian refugees – and had stayed. She arrived one day on Iona, announcing that she wished 'to see Iona and sing some old Scots songs before I die'! Her community had given her the train fare to the French coast. Heaven knows how she'd got across the Channel. Once in Britain, she borrowed money from her family here to get to Iona. We had an amazing three days with her; she was tremendous fun, charmed everyone. As she was leaving, she told me: 'You know, Mr Harvey, I have manic depression. I spend about six months of every year in hospital. Mostly, I feel suicidal. But of course I don't do it – my faith doesn't allow it, you see.' What a witness!

John Harvey, a member of the Iona Community

Just nearby stands:

THE FONT

This font was placed in the Abbey in the early part of the last century. To be baptised (Christened) signifies a decision to be a follower, a disciple, of Jesus. Water is poured over whoever is baptised, symbolising being washed clean, and a willingness to live by Christ's standards.

Think of things you have done, or not done, that you regret. In your imagination, place them in the font.

Prayer

O God,
pour your Spirit over me,
wash me clean.
Help me to turn
from wrong ways of living.

May God forgive you, Christ renew you,
and the Spirit enable you to grow in love.

A STORY

I first came to Iona in 1958, fresh out of the army from national service. I had been brought up in a Christian tradition which was a mixture of conservative evangelicalism and middle-of-the-road Presbyterianism. Iona blew my mind. A combination of the history of the place – I suppose I had thought that Christianity probably started in Scotland around 1560! – and the excitement of the Iona Community really started me on the road to a new faith. For the first time I met an expression of Christianity that made the link between worship and world, set within the fullness of universal Christianity, in a way that was both accessible and challenging to me. For me, this was like being born again.

John Harvey, a member of the Iona Community

THE TOMBSTONES OF THE BISHOP AND THE ABBOT

Near the font, against a wall, are some tombstones, brought inside from the Reilig Odhráin to protect them from further erosion. Notice the staffs on the tombstones of the bishop and the abbot.

The bishop's crook is turned outwards, signifying blessing the active work in the world. The abbot's crook is turned inwards – a blessing on the inner life. The living tradition here in Iona Abbey sees all of our life, inner and outer, as integral to the expression of our faith.

Think of the work you do – at home, in a factory or an office, at school or college ... Where do you find relaxation? When do you find a chance to be quiet?

Prayer

Hold the balance,
God who made me.
May work be one,
play be one,
reflection be one.
Three-in-one God
make me whole.

Look down from the top of the nave steps and notice the straight line between the paving stones near the foot of the steps.

THE LINE OF THE NAVE'S EXTENSION

The nave was extended in the thirteenth and fourteenth centuries. Communities have different needs and different priorities in worship at different times. Church reordering today can generate conflicting passions between those who worship and those who want to preserve an historic building. The changes in the interior of the Abbey reflect the faith priorities of worshipping communities at different times, built upon the priorities of past generations. Just as homes built to the same plan look very different inside, reflecting something of the people living in them, so too do the churches of worshipping communities.

Take a moment to think of the different communities you belong to – at home, work, school, or church; locally, nationally and around the world. What do the buildings they use say about them?

Prayer

Far-seeing God,
enlarge our vision
to fit your purposes
and reflect your glory.

As you move down the nave, further into the church, look at the floor again.

THE CIRCLES OF PEBBLES IN THE NAVE FLOOR

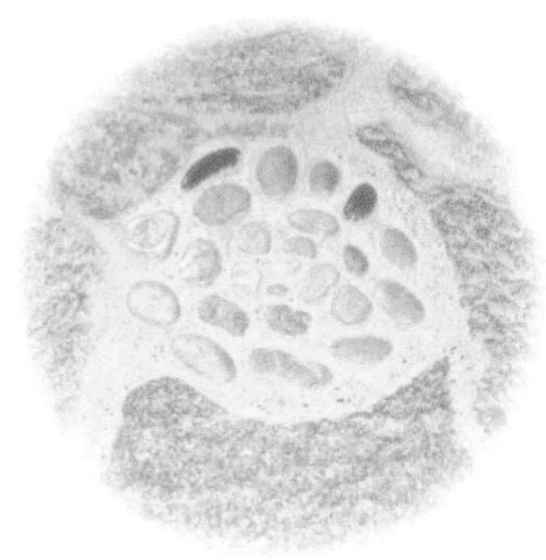

During building work in the early twentieth century, skeletons of monks buried underneath the Abbey floor were discovered. Beside some of the monks were little piles of pebbles. It is thought that each pebble represented a year of the monk's life in the monastery. Crosses and circles of pebbles laid in the Abbey floor mark the sites of these graves.

Just for a moment, remember the monks of the past and the model of faithful Christian life they represent. Then recall someone close to you who has died and whose life inspired you.

Prayer

God the harvester,
You gathered ....
into Your barn.
Thank You for
the life s/he lived,
the model shown.
May the seed
scattered within me
bear much grain.

Facing the leader's desk, stand under the tower in the crossing and look up.

THE NORTH TRANSEPT ARCH

The original, smaller thirteenth-century arch was too weak to support the fifteenth-century tower, so a stronger arch was built underneath it. Look near the floor for a base of the original pillars.

Think of the times when you have been glad of the support of others, and when others have been glad of your support. We are not meant to struggle alone.

Prayer

God bless you,
friends and strangers who held me;
    through trouble,
    through fear,
    through trembling weakness.

Christ within you
be also in me,
    when you cry out,
    when you flounder,
    when you crack under pressure;
that, in Christ's strength,
our weaknesses
may support towers
that sing of God's glory.

Stand in the leader's desk and look at the archway on your right, and the pillar on the left side of that arch. Look up the pillar to see:

THE HOWLING FACE IN THE STONEWORK

It is thought that this carving represents the face of a man tormented in hell, clearly so desperately thirsty that his tongue is hanging out. This carving was placed opposite the pulpit probably to remind the preacher of his (as it was in those days) responsibility to proclaim the gospel for the saving of his listeners from hell. The carving is placed where it is to work as a form of ancient public address system by encouraging the preacher project his voice the better to be heard throughout the church. Latterly tour guides have suggested that it may have been placed there to remind the preacher not to go on for too long!

Ideas and emphases change with time and with culture. Think of the most important changes in your ideas in your own spiritual search.

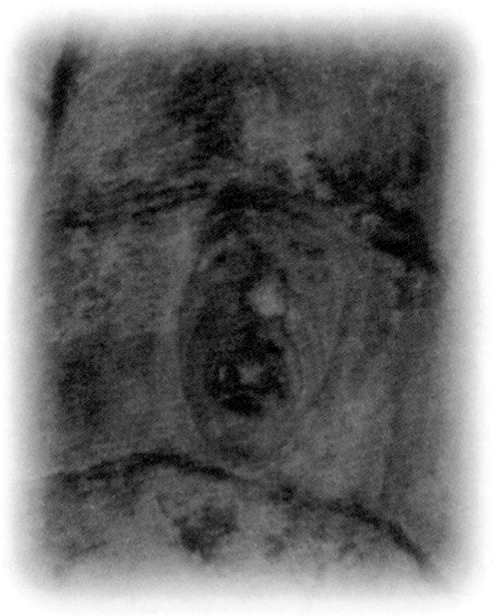

Prayer

God,
lead us from death to life, from falsehood to truth.
Lead us from despair to hope, from fear to trust.
Lead us from hate to love, from war to peace.
Let peace fill our hearts, our world, our universe.
We ask it for your own name's sake. Amen

Universal prayer for peace, from *Iona Abbey Worship Book*

Cross over to the Argyll Memorial in the south transept.

TWO PEOPLE OF VISION

Behind the metal screen lie the effigies of George Douglas Campbell, the eighth Duke of Argyll, and his wife, Ina, Duchess of Argyll. In 1899 the Duke of Argyll, probably at the instigation of his wife, who loved Iona and often visited the island, established a trust for the rebuilding and preservation of the Abbey church. The trust deed included a specific provision for the Abbey to be made available as 'a place of worship for Christians of all traditions' – an act of courage and vision at a time when antagonism was felt by some towards members of other denominations. The Iona Community is an ecumenical community and has made it a priority to seek the unity of the divided Church.

Take a moment to think of groups you belong to. How do they – and how do you – find the resources to refresh vision and experience renewal?

Where there is no vision the people perish.
Proverbs 29:18

Prayer

Holy Spirit,
You nurture us and You want us to grow.
Lead us in Your wild dance,
so that we may tread the unfamiliar paths
singing gladly,
and find fulfilment for the dreams
that fit Your knowing of us.

Look for the cross carved on the east wall of the duke and duchess's memorial.

THE CONSECRATION CROSS

This cross was made in the thirteenth century to show that the church was consecrated for worship. In baptism every new Christian has the sign of the cross made on their forehead. Both the consecration cross and the cross made in baptism are simple crosses that signify a purpose.

Remember your own commitments and think of God's purposes for you.

Prayer

Your will, O God, be done.
Not mine, with my desire for security,
for comfort – and anything for a quiet life.

Your will, O God, be done.
Not mine, which gets so mixed up
with fear and anger,
with wayward hurt feelings –
and wishes, Lord –
mixed up with wishes is my will.
For pleasure and wealth – to win, to succeed,
to be happy.

Bring my will in line with Yours.
My will alongside Yours.
So that when I say
'Your will be done',

it is mine too.

Face the Argyll Memorial then turn left. Here you enter the south aisle. Right at the end of the south aisle is a small side chapel, where many visitors and pilgrims have prayed before you.

THE PRAYER CORNER IN THE SOUTH AISLE CHAPEL

From its beginning the Iona Community has felt drawn by God to engage in the ministry of healing. On a window ledge in the prayer corner is a wooden box, and on Tuesday evenings, during a healing service, prayers are offered for the healing of those whose names are placed in this box. You are welcome to leave names there; paper and pens are provided.

Also in the South Aisle Chapel is a stand of candles.

Light a candle for something that concerns you: a personal situation or one in the world community; for someone you know who needs healing of body, mind or spirit, or for your own needs.

Prayer

Living God,
bring your light
to the shadows and darknesses
of our lives together.
Set your blessing on *(a person, a place, a problem)*
that your peace and healing may be known.

Living God,
enlighten our hearts with your love,
our minds with your truth,
our bodies with your grace.
Especially help ....
That s/he may know your healing.

Candles in the Abbey

Some candles flickered in a downdraft;
some stood still,
lighting, in orange flame, the precious dark.

Their silence created silence;
their dimness in so vast a space
soothed the restless soul.

Their light was a quiet presence
that spoke of *the* light, the real presence,
come to meet us at the appointed place.

He was there, though human eyes
are not given to see him.
Hearts, open to receive him, rested a while
in a circle of peace.

David Levison, a member of the Iona Community

Look up at the larger window in the South Aisle Chapel and notice the trefoil patterns in the top circle.

THE EAST WINDOW OF THE SOUTH AISLE CHAPEL

There are many trinity symbols in the Abbey. Another can be seen in the top circle of the window over the communion table. Knowing God as the Holy Trinity – as Creator, Son and Holy Spirit, three-in-one – reveals the relationship *within* God into which we too are invited and welcomed.

Celtic prayer, ancient and modern, frequently reflects this way of relating to God, and we are deeply enriched by coming to know God in this manner.

To pray this way yourself, take up the concern that came to mind earlier in the South Aisle Chapel.

Pray with that concern to God the Holy Spirit to guide you and give you the wisdom you need.

Pray with the concern to Jesus, God the Son, who walks beside you and knows the struggles and joys of human living, and who is there with you as you face conflict, illness, or any other problem.

Pray in confidence to God the Creator, who made you and all the world, that the same creative energy may flow through you.

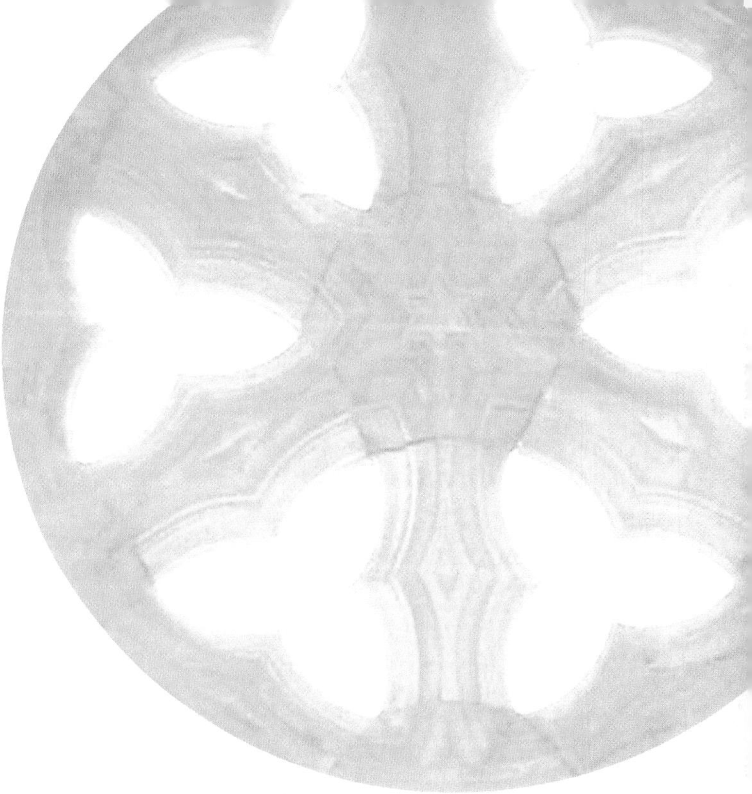

Prayer

In name of Father,
In name of Son,
In name of Spirit,
    Three in One:

Father cherish me,
Son cherish me,
Spirit cherish me,
    Three all-kindly.

God make me holy,
Christ make me holy,
Spirit make me holy,
    Three all-holy.

Three aid my hope,
Three aid my love,
Three aid mine eye,
    And my knee from stumbling,
    My knee from stumbling.

A traditional Celtic prayer, from the *Carmina Gadelica*

In the South Aisle Chapel you will find a small picture of St Columba.

THE ICON OF ST COLUMBA

We are indebted to Adomnán, Abbot of Iona from 679–704, for giving us in his *Life of Columba* most of the facts we know about the saint, whose zeal for the Church, together with his gentleness and sincerity of soul, earned for him his name, which means 'Dove'.

The narrative elements of Columba's life can be easily read in the icon. The boat signifies Columba's voluntary exile from Ireland; the oak leaves incorporated into his halo recall Doire (Derry), his beloved oak grove. The Celtic crosses denote the saint's monastic foundations prior to his famous one on Iona.

Adomnán praises Columba's devotion to the scriptures, which he loved to copy. His love for the psalms in particular is signified by the text in the open book: 'Come let us rejoice in the Lord, with songs let us praise Him.' (Psalm 94)

The white horse in the icon is mentioned in Adomnán's account of Columba, where the monastery horse, sensing the last day of the saint's life, came to him and wept tears into Columba's lap.

In an icon, however, if we consider only the narrative elements we remain on the surface and miss their deeper spiritual meanings. In the legend of the horse we are being taught to respect and love all God's creatures. The boat, too, has a deeper symbolism – of the church, the barque of Peter, whose teaching the saint proclaimed. And the book is the Word of God Himself to whom Columba was so devoted. Hills in an icon, as in the Bible, are always holy places, an ascent to God; and here our ascent to where Columba stands is made easier for us by being stepped, with each step edged with helpful light.

Before the icon our gaze gradually changes. From being the one who is looking, we become the one who is being seen. Columba's steady compassionate gaze denotes his full attention as we ask for his help. His right hand holds aloft not a sword as on the insignia of the O'Donnell clan, of which he was a royal prince, but a cross, the symbol of reconciliation.

This, coupled with the broken sword under his feet, strongly emphasises the appeal for peace in Columba's dying words to his disciples – as relevant today as in those turbulent times:

'May you always have among you mutual charity and peace.'

Sister Aloysius McVeigh, icon painter

Think of the people who have been important to you in your spiritual journey.

Prayer

Christ, draw near to us,
little people, trembling and most wretched,
rowing through the infinite storm
of this age;
and bring us safely
to the most beautiful haven of life.

Attributed to St Columba

Move into the chancel now. If you look up at the walls around the communion table you will see ferns growing.

THE FERNS GROWING IN THE WALL

These ferns are an amazing example of the surprises and resilience of creation. They live on the moisture absorbed by the particular mix of mortar between the stones. Creation is God-breathed, and the care of creation a natural response to God.

Take time to look at the ferns and the stones around them.

Prayer

God of surprises,
in the dry cracks
of my heart and soul,
breathe your life,
green and growing,
defying probability,
proclaiming hope.

Beneath the ferns on the south wall lies the effigy of Abbot Dominic.

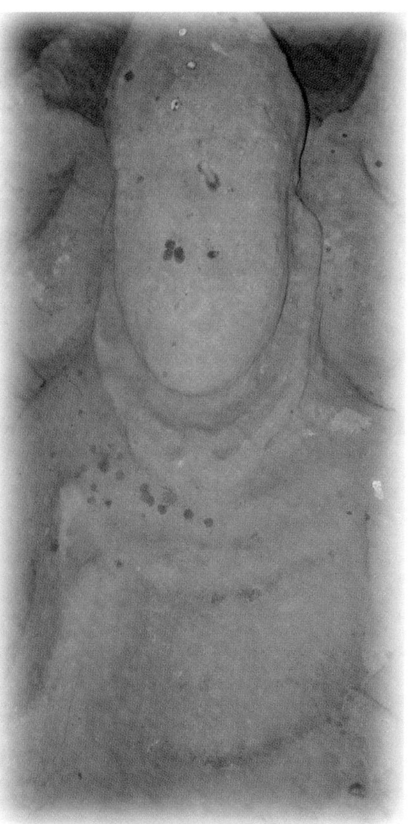

THE CONTINUING RENEWAL OF THE CHURCH

A reforming abbot of the fifteenth century, Abbot Dominic worked for the renewal of the Abbey building as well as for the spiritual life of the community of his day. The monks had become very slack, as all human groups at times do, and Abbot Dominic encouraged them to work and pray for their renewal and for that of the Church.

Take time to pray for the renewal of the Church.

PRAYER

Draw us to Jesus, O God,
that we may draw closer
to each other.

So may the building arise,
stone upon stone,
grounded on love.

Look for the inscription '*I AM THE BREAD OF LIFE*' carved on the right-hand end of the communion table.

THE COMMUNION TABLE

The communion table is carved from Iona marble, which was quarried at the southern end of the island until early in the twentieth century. Marble is a metamorphic rock, which is to say that the original minerals have been changed by intense heat and pressure – several times in the case of this marble. Run your hands over the stone. Feel the cracks and flaws. Look closely at the green streaks of serpentine. Compare this to the flawless white marble used in the Argyll Memorial. The beauty of Iona marble lies in its imperfection. This is indeed a 'sermon in stone'; for here, at the very heart of our weekly worship, is a reminder that, in the offering of our lives, as in the offering of bread and wine, God's Spirit works in transformation.

Jesus took the ordinary staple food of life and made it holy.

Prayer of consecration

Hear us, O Christ,
and breathe your Spirit upon us
and upon this bread and wine.
May they become for us your body,
vibrant with your life,
healing, renewing and making us whole.
And as the bread and wine which we now eat and drink
are changed into us,
may we be changed again into you,
bone of your bone,
flesh of your flesh,
loving and caring in the world.

From *Iona Abbey Worship Book*

Behind the communion table stands the silver Celtic cross.

THE SILVER CELTIC CROSS

The Celtic cross is a resurrection cross: Jesus is risen, so there is no figure, and the cross on the circle of the world is a cross of glory. The cross and circle together create a new pattern. Because of the resurrection we see the cross differently (though do not deny its pain), and in our lives we can recognise joy through the pain.

Pause and think of the smaller resurrections you have known.

Prayer

Living God,
your light changes the view,
reflects a deeper pattern,
makes sense of the shadows,
sets rainbows against storm clouds.
Open my eyes and heart
to see your resurrection
touch all about me.
Alleluia

A STORY

David Russell had invited George to go with him to Hampstead, where there was an exhibition and sale of silver work of the late Omar Ramsden, so that George could choose a piece suitable for Iona. He saw the wonderful cross in the midst, but did not like to ask for the most important thing in the show, so he pretended to be looking at chalices.

'You're really looking at the cross, aren't you, George?' observed Dr Russell. When they asked about it, Ramsden's widow told them it was not for sale because her husband, who considered it his finest work – it had been displayed at the Empire Exhibition in Glasgow in 1938 – had intended that it would stand in Iona Abbey one day ...

Ron Ferguson, from *George MacLeod: Founder of the Iona Community*

To the right of the communion table, as you face it, you will see carved faces on the sedilia ('little seat'). The sedilia is where the priest sat during the parts of the service when he wasn't standing at the communion table.

THE FACES ON THE SEDILIA

There are weathered and indistinguishable faces, and one that is restored and clear. The faces tell a story of the effects of wind and rain when the Abbey was in ruins, and of careful restoration.

Our own faces tell a story. Sit here and consider your own story.

PRAYER

God the Maker,
thank you for making me
just as I am.

Jesus the Christ,
show me your footprints
beside me each day.

Spirit so Holy,
bless and enable
the journey to come.

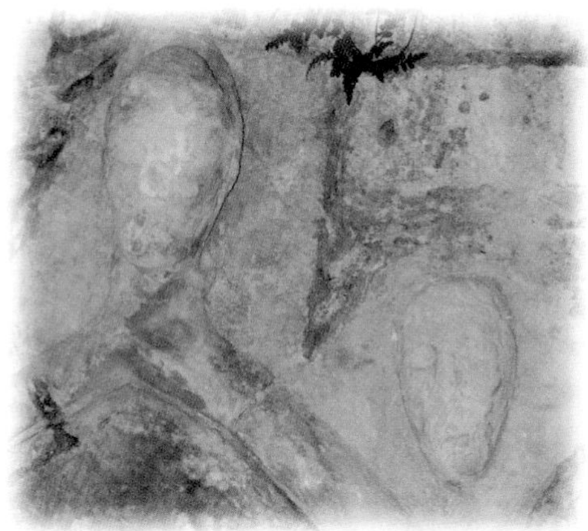

On the wall above you, look for two animals, a monkey and a cat (somewhat weathered now), carved on either side of the window.

THE MONKEY AND THE CAT

The monkey represents the active and busy side of life; the cat reminds us of the stillness of contemplation. Usually we think of the active side of life belonging outside the church but here both sides of the Christian spiritual journey are placed in the sanctuary, by the communion table. The rhythm of work and prayer, action and contemplation, was the monastic lifestyle for both the Benedictines and the Columban monks before them.

If you walk down into the choir, and back round towards the Duke of Argyll's memorial, you will see (on the capital of a pillar) where the original stonemasons have carved a bullock or a cow being brought to slaughter.

Christian folk in the past didn't leave all their 'worldly' concerns at the church door.
How does it feel to think of all the different parts of your life belonging here in this place?

Prayer

Grant us, Lord, that balance
of action and stillness,
of work and play
that fits the wholeness you intend for us.
Help us to see that all is prayer;
all things part of life with You.

Turn and face the crossing, then move over to the north transept.

THE NORTH TRANSEPT

The stairs in the north transept lead to the residential part of the Abbey and were the night stairs for the Benedictine monks, connecting the part of the Abbey where the Benedictines lived with their place of prayer. For the Benedictines prayer, work and even sleep were interwoven. Part of the rule of the present-day Iona Community is a commitment to 'action for justice and peace'. The community tries to follow in the footsteps of, among others, Adomnán, the early, Celtic Abbot of Iona who wrote the *Life of Columba* and was called 'liberator of the women of the Gaels'. Inspired by stories of Columba's protection of the innocent, Adomnán introduced a law to protect women and non-combatants in the time of battle. The issues highlighted in the north transept may not be comfortable ones, but they speak of the needs of God's children around the world.

Take time to look at the justice and peace material displayed here. Think of the need for justice and peace where you live or work, and draw it into your prayer.

Prayer

God give us peace,
but not at the expense
of those who are hungry
or whose labour is exploited;

not so dictators kill and torture
or armies bully and destroy;

not so some are excluded
for others to be comfortable.

Give us peace with Your justice.
So Your Kin-dom will come,
Your will be done.

A story

I can never come down the stairs into the north transept without thinking of our predecessors here – the Benedictine monks of the thirteenth to fifteenth centuries. I know these aren't the actual stairs they used, but near here they came down, night after night, summer and winter, into the Abbey church to say the night office. No central heating, no electric light – just doing it, doing the 'work of God', as they saw it, because that was what they had committed themselves to. When we used to feel sorry for ourselves (as I guess people still do from time to time up on Iona!) – too busy, stressed, not coping, fed up with guests or day tourists or just ourselves – I used to think of these anonymous monks coming down that night stair, heavy with sleep, and ... well, just give myself a shake. We stand in a great tradition of commitment – and the daily, nightly 'work of God', whatever it may be.

John Harvey, a member of the Iona Community

'THE CRUCIFIXION' BY LE MAISTRE

The painting 'The Crucifixion' by R. Le Maistre, which hangs here in the north transept, portrays our Lord in the moment after he had cried, 'It is finished!' Jesus has faithfully completed his task. It is appropriate that this painting should hang here among the materials campaigning for the rights of political prisoners and others who are oppressed and exploited.

Our Lord's task is completed. Our tasks remain. Take a moment to reflect, perhaps with the help of the materials available, on your own vocation to serve.

Prayer

Lord Jesus, you hung upon the cross for our salvation. We watch with amazement and gratitude from the foot of the cross.

Lord Jesus, you bowed your head for the salvation of the world. Help us to pick up our cross and follow you into the world.

Amen

Leave the church now and go out into the cloisters. The cloisters provided a covered way for getting from the residential buildings to the church and back. Cloisters are traditionally a place for meditation or meeting and conversation. Just two of the original cloister pillars survive. Christopher Hall, the principal cloister sculptor, and Douglas Bisset undertook the twentieth-century carvings, which portray images of the plants of the Holy Land and the British Isles, plants and birds of Iona and some Christian symbols:

THE ORIGINAL CLOISTER PILLARS

Old and weathered as they are, these pillars still give the pattern and design for all the rest.

The faith of the past is constantly remade and renewed, old and new side by side. Think of yourself for a moment as the very place where that renewal is under way.

Prayer

God of the ages;
Jesus, yesterday, today and for ever;
Spirit breathing life since the dawn of creation;
give us courage to walk new paths with You;
open our eyes to the endless depths
of Your mystery.

A STORY

My son, Roddie, and I stood in the cloister watching a young man excavating the southeast corner, where there is a little bit of masonry projecting through the grass. In those days it had been supporting a water butt catching rain from the roof of the joiner's hut. We knew already that it was all that was left of the church destroyed by the Danes. Its foundations can be traced under the floor of the Abbey church.

'I think you've got a skull there,' I said.

'Lots of skulls in Iona,' he replied, putting his spade in again.

'There's another,' I said. So he continued more carefully.

Around the corner of masonry he uncovered the bones of a mass burial.

It did not take long to establish that they were men, young men (wisdom teeth not through yet in some cases), having died with violently smashed skulls. And one lad had his little finger between his teeth, and his lower jaw had been driven right up into his upper jaw.

Pieces of burnt wattle came to light, reminding us that the church had been burnt down. The bodies of the occupants had been laid out round the wall of the ruined building, which would have then have been upset over them. That was a common way of burying people after a battle in those days. From then on we called that place 'the skullery'.

Ian Cowie
Originally published in *Columba's Island* by E. Mairi MacArthur

Notice the carvings on the capitals of the pillars at the four corners of the cloisters. They represent passages from the Bible: Alpha and Omega, the raising of Lazarus, sharing bread and wine, and the parable of the mustard seed.

CLOISTER CARVING (ALPHA AND OMEGA)

One of the carvings is of a face surrounded by knotwork and scrolling plants, hair flowing out like water. Alpha and Omega are the first and last letters of the Greek alphabet. In the Book of Revelation Christ calls himself the Alpha and Omega, the beginning and the end.

Think of your own beginnings and endings.

Prayer

God, Maker;
God, Lover of Souls;
God, Inspirer;
help me to see,
through all my moments,
that you are there,
my beginning and my end.

A STORY

Campbell Saunders and I, as new members of the Iona Community in the summer of 1952, were creating a cloister pavement a year ahead of the flagstones being officially laid in their permanent position, when George MacLeod came through the gate. 'Good,' he said, surveying our work. 'Aye,' said Campbell, 'it's all right for *some*.' 'Are you referring to me, Saunders?' said George. 'I'm referring to *you*, MacLeod,' said Campbell. We all three roared with laughter. George and Campbell got into a bear hug and tumbled and rolled over in mock combat. Like a grandfather larking with his grandchildren – the great man delighted in the humour of the situation.

Bob Currie, a member of the Iona Community

CLOISTER CARVING (SHARING THE BREAD AND WINE)

The hands of Jesus broke bread and shared wine with the disciples on the night before he died. And Christians do this in the communion service, thanking God for Jesus's self-giving.

Where have you known brokenness in your life?

PRAYER

Help me to see
that only what is broken
can be shared;
that we can only share the wine
that has been poured out.
Help us to share our bread and our lives.

BE STILL

Look for the bench with the words 'BE STILL' carved on its backrest.

Here, unexpected, is a phrase from Psalm 46: 'Be still and know that I am God.'

Take time to be still and listen.

Prayer

Hear the quiet of Iona ... and echo it in the stillness of your heart:

at every turn,
wherever you are,
unexpected,
God says BE STILL.

In the centre of the cloisters you will see a modernist sculpture by Jacob Lipschitz, a Lithuanian Jew who studied in Paris; it is one of three sculptures given to places of Christian renewal by Mrs J. Owen in 1956.

THE DESCENT OF THE SPIRIT

The sculpture represents the incarnation: the coming of God in human form through the Virgin Mary. Mary is supported by three angels as the Holy Spirit surrounds and fills her. Both Mary and the lamb are blind. Only the dove, a symbol for the Holy Spirit, has huge open eyes. The lamb reminds us of Jesus's death on the cross.

The modern Iona Community is an ecumenical group of women and men from different walks of life and different traditions of the Church, committed to seeking new ways of living the gospel of Jesus Christ in today's world. The figure of the Virgin reminds us of what was lost to the Protestant expression of the Christian faith in the upheaval of the Reformation. Because it is the work of a Jewish artist, the sculpture also reminds us of the burning need for reconciliation between the great world faiths.

The inscription reads:

Jacob Lipschitz, Juif fidèle
À la foi de ses ancêtres
A fait cette vierge pour
La bonne entente des
Hommes sur la terre à fin
Que l'Esprit règne

Jacob Lipschitz, a Jew faithful
To the belief of his ancestors
Made this Virgin for
The good understanding of
People on earth in order
That the Spirit might reign

Think of friends or neighbours whose tradition or belief or lifestyle is different from your own.

Prayer

Holy Spirit,
Enemy of apathy,
Dove of peace,
Lady Wisdom,
open my eyes to the
unseen purposes of God.

Disturb me in those purposes I see
but do not follow
and bless me in those I do.

A STORY

I had to give up one of my two weeks of honeymoon to complete Iona Community membership training. George arranged that I should be in the youth hut and Margaret, my wife, in the village! We were in the cloisters in their ruined state, when a man with a camera approached us and asked if he might take a couple of photographs. Having done this, he said that a time would come when the photos would be needed. Fifty years later we were asked for a photo of our start to married life for a book!

Ian M Fraser, a member of the Iona Community

There are more things to see in the Abbey museum, which is reached by going round to the back of the Abbey. The only way to get to Iona is by boat. You will have reached Iona by ferry. You will find another kind of boat carved on a cross shaft there.

THE CARVING OF THE GALLEY IN THE ABBEY MUSEUM
(LACHLAN AND JOHN MACKINNON'S CROSS)

This carving is of a medieval West Highland galley, which was based on the design of earlier Viking longships. The Vikings journeyed to Iona, killing many of the Columban monks, making them martyrs. One of the bays of Iona is called Martyrs' Bay.

The Celtic monks let themselves be carried by the tides in their little coracles, believing that God would guide them. In one story, a crew threw away their oars and landed safely on the distant shores of Cornwall! This total faith and trust in God converted a local king there.

Think of the journeys ahead of you.

Prayer

God of the journey,
make us always willing
to set out afresh,
ready to be surprised
and open to new directions,
new perspectives.

THE INFIRMARY

The museum was once the site of the Abbey infirmary, where the sick were cared for and found healing. We hope that you find healing on your pilgrimage here.

Prayer

The blessing of God
on your journey here.
The love of the Maker be yours,
the peace of the Christ be yours,
the healing of the Spirit be yours.
The blessing of God
on your journey here
and on the path ahead.
Amen

A story

One St Columba's Day, there was a short pilgrimage, as an act of evening worship, from the Abbey to the pier. We were, as so often, joined in this by a number of visitors to the island. One visitor came up to me after the service and said: 'I am so grateful that you have had an act of worship in which I felt able to join. I am claustrophobic. I can never enter a church building for worship – but I have been able to join you this evening. Thank you very much for that.' This relates to journeys ahead or, rather, to going out from the Abbey into the world.

Graeme Brown, a member of the Iona Community

Blessing

May God be a bright flame before you,
be a guiding star above you,
be a smooth path below you,
be a kindly shepherd behind you,
today, tomorrow and for ever.

A traditional Gaelic blessing, from *Iona Abbey Worship Book*

ACKNOWLEDGEMENTS:

Several Iona Community members helped to write this guide. Thanks especially to:

Graeme Brown

Bob Currie

Ron Ferguson

Ian M Fraser

John Harvey

David Levison

Kate McIlhagga

Tony Phelan

Richard Sharples

Jean Young

PRAYERS:

'Holy Spirit, awaken my heart …' – by Chris Polhill

'Eternal God, You bring life out of death …' – by Chris Polhill

'May the desire of my heart …' – by Chris Pohill

'When we are happy …' (from 'Welcome') – by Kate McIlhagga, from *The Green Heart of the Snowdrop*, p.19, Kate McIlhagga, Wild Goose Publications, 2004. ISBN 1901557855. © Donald McIlhagga.

'O God, pour your Spirit over me …' – by Neil Paynter and Chris Polhill

'May God forgive you, Christ renew you …' – from *Iona Abbey Worship Book*, Wild Goose Publications, 2001. ISBN 1901557502.

'Hold the balance ...' – by Chris Polhill

'Far-seeing God ...' – by Chris Polhill

'God the harvester ...' – by Chris Polhill

'God bless you, friends and strangers who held me ...' – by Chris Polhill

'Holy Spirit, You nurture us and you want us to grow ...' – by Chris Polhill

'Your will, O God, be done ...' – by Chris Polhill

'Living God, bring your light ...' – by Chris Polhill

'God of surprises ...' – by Chris Polhill

'Draw us to Jesus ...' – by Graeme Brown

'Living God, your light changes the view ...' – by Chris Polhill

'God the Maker ...' – by Chris Polhill

'Grant us, Lord, that balance of action and stillness ...' – by Chris Polhill

'God give us peace ...' – by Chris Polhill

'Lord Jesus, you hung upon the cross for our salvation ...' – by Graeme Brown

'God of the ages ...' – by Tony Phelan

'God, Maker ...' – by Tony Phelan

'Help me to see ...' – by Tony Phelan

'Hear the quiet of Iona ...' – by Tony Phelan

'Holy Spirit, Enemy of apathy ...' – by Chris Polhill

'God of the journey ...' – by Tony Phelan

'The blessing of God on your journey here ...' – by Chris Polhill

PHOTOGRAPHS:

The cloisters – Chris Polhill

Rainbow – David Coleman

Iona Abbey – David Coleman

St Martin's Cross – Chris Polhill

The Street of the Dead – Chris Polhill

Tòrr an Aba – Neil Paynter

St John's Cross – Chris Polhill

The watching place – Chris Polhill

The font – Chris Polhill

Tombstones of the bishop and abbot – Neil Paynter

Circle of pebbles – Chris Polhill

North transept arch – Chris Polhill

The howling face – Neil Paynter

Effigy of the Eighth Duke of Argyll – Chris Polhill

Consecration cross – Neil Paynter

South aisle chapel – Chris Polhill

Stand of candles – Chris Polhill

Candles in the Abbey – David Coleman

East window of the South aisle chapel – Chris Polhill

Icon of St Columba – Icon painted by Sister Aloysius McVeigh; reproduced from a print of the icon.

Fern – Neil Paynter

Abbot Dominic – Neil Paynter

I am the bread – Chris Polhill

Silver Celtic cross – Chris Polhill

Faces on the sedilia – Chris Polhill

Monkey and cat – Based on material from Royal Commission on Ancient and Historical Monuments of Scotland. Used by permission of RCAHMS.

R. De Maistre's painting of 'The Crucifixion' – Martin Grashoff

Alpha and the Omega (cloister carving by Chris Hall) – Chris Polhill

Sharing the bread (cloister carving by Chris Hall) – Chris Polhill

Be still – Chris Polhill

Boat in the museum (Lachlan and John MacKinnon's cross) – Neil Paynter

The Descent of the Spirit by Jacob Lipschitz – David Coleman

The Iona Community is:

- An ecumenical movement of men and women from different walks of life and different traditions in the Christian church
- Committed to the gospel of Jesus Christ, and to following where that leads, even into the unknown
- Engaged together, and with people of goodwill across the world, in acting, reflecting and praying for justice, peace and the integrity of creation
- Convinced that the inclusive community we seek must be embodied in the community we practise

Together with our staff, we are responsible for:

- Our islands residential centres of Iona Abbey, the MacLeod Centre on Iona, and Camas Adventure Centre on the Ross of Mull

and in Glasgow:

- The administration of the Community
- Our work with young people
- Our publishing house, Wild Goose Publications
- Our association in the revitalising of worship with the Wild Goose Resource Group

The Iona Community was founded in Glasgow in 1938 by George MacLeod, minister, visionary and prophetic witness for peace, in the context of the poverty and despair of the Depression. Its original task of rebuilding the monastic ruins of Iona Abbey became a sign of hopeful rebuilding of community in Scotland and beyond. Today, we are about 250 Members, mostly in Britain, and 1500 Associate Members, with 1400 Friends worldwide. Together and apart, 'we follow the light we have, and pray for more light'.

For information on the Iona Community contact:
The Iona Community, Fourth Floor, Savoy House, 140 Sauchiehall Street, Glasgow G2 3DH, UK. Phone: 0141 332 6343
e-mail: ionacomm@gla.iona.org.uk; web: www.iona.org.uk

For enquiries about visiting Iona, please contact:
Iona Abbey, Isle of Iona, Argyll PA76 6SN, UK. Phone: 01681 700404
e-mail: ionacomm@iona.org.uk

Also from Wild Goose Publications:

THE CLOISTERS OF IONA ABBEY

Ewan Mathers

A collection of beautiful photographs depicting in detail the carvings of the restored cloisters of Iona Abbey, with text reflecting on the meaning of each design and information about the flora and fauna of the Isle of Iona and beyond which most of the carvings represent. The author, a frequent visitor to Iona since childhood, observed the newly built cloisters being transformed over thirty years from rough pillars of sandstone into a complete, unified work of art. From his own obsession with the carvings and conversations with their main creator, Chris Hall, has emerged the concept of cloisters as a labyrinth, the winding circular pathway on ancient mythology, the purpose of which was to effect a change of consciousness.

ISBN 1 901557 60 X

DVD: THE IONA COMMUNITY & SERMON IN STONE

Contains two very informative films about the Iona Community, together with an update by its current leader, Kathy Galloway. *The Iona Community: Today's Challenge, Tomorrow's Hope* was filmed in 2000 and gives a good idea of life and work at the community's centres on Iona and at Camas, where hundreds of visitors are welcomed each year. It also portrays some of the organisation's activities on the mainland. *Sermon in Stone* was made during the 1960s and has not been widely available for some time. It includes film from the archives of the Iona Community and shows the reconstruction of Iona Abbey from the late 1930s until the end of the 1960s. George MacLeod, the founder of the community, features prominently.

ISBN 1 905010 07 9

IONA ABBEY WORSHIP BOOK

The Iona Community

The services and resources in this book reflect the Iona Community's commitment to the belief that worship is all that we are and all that we do, both inside and outside the church, with no division into the 'sacred' and the 'secular'. They draw on many traditions, including the Celtic, and aim to help us to be fully present to God, who is fully present to us – in our neighbour, in the political and social activity of the world around us, and in the very centre and soul of our being.

ISBN 1 901557 50 2

GEORGE MACLEOD: FOUNDER OF THE IONA COMMUNITY

Ron Ferguson

Born just before the start of the 20th century into a famous ecclesiastical dynasty, George MacLeod became disturbed by his increasing awareness of 'two nations', the rich and the poor, while working as a young minister in Edinburgh during the 1920s and shocked his many admirers by taking a post as a minister in Govan, a poor and depressed area of Glasgow. Although he had been awarded the Military Cross and the Croix de Guerre for bravery during the war, he moved inexorably towards socialism and pacifism during the Depression years, while his theology evolved in mystical, cosmic and political directions. In 1938, feeling that a radical move was necessary to meet the needs of the times, MacLeod embarked on the imaginative venture of rebuilding part of the ancient abbey on the isle of Iona. He utilised the skills of unemployed craftsmen, and persuaded trainee ministers to work as labourers. Out of this was born the often controversial Iona Community, which over the years has trained clergy for work in deprived areas, produced innovative worship for the world church, pleaded for disarmament, inveighed against world hunger and advocated joint ecumenical action on social issues.

ISBN 1 901557 53 7